MOTHER TERESA ON ADVENT AND CHRISTMAS

John Scally

Mother Teresa
on Advent and Christmas

the columba press

First published in 2014 by

the columba press

55A Spruce Avenue, Stillorgan Industrial Park,
Blackrock, Co. Dublin

Cover image by Kalai Selvam
Cover design by David Mc Namara CSsR
Origination by The Columba Press
Printed by ScandBook AB, Sweden

ISBN 978 1 78218 195 8

Acknowledgements
I am grateful to John Littleton and Raphael Beuthner for their support.
Thanks to Patrick, Michael and all at Columba.
Special thanks to the amazing Sandra Mooney for her ongoing inspiration.

Contents

Introduction

In her remarkable life, Mother Teresa left an enduring imprint on the conscience and consciousness of the world because of her compassion and her work for the poor. This tiny Albanian nun, winner of the Nobel Peace Prize, with her hands joined in the Indian gesture of greeting, taught the world the meaning of compassion. Her name was synonymous with 'doing good'. Diana, Princess of Wales, regarded her a friend and a saint. Throughout her life, anything worth doing for the poor was worth doing, no matter what the cost. She was conscious of what she called her 'uselessness', her 'emptiness'. While renowned for her focus on the poor, she was equally devoted to the Eucharist and concentrated on adoration of the Blessed Sacrament, prayer, contemplation and study. She believed in St Augustine's idea of 'mingling mercy with misery'.

Mother Teresa did not simply preach compassion — she lived it. She made personal, intimate contact in her daily life with those rejected by society: the homeless, prisoners, the sick, the dying, the old, and the lonely. Not only did she devote her life to marginalised people, but she inspired others to follow her and, most importantly, by her love and attention to them, she rendered the invisible people of the world visible; she brought the most brutalised, rejected and marginalised people of the world to the centre of the stage. She showed us, not only that the rejected ones of society need our love and our help, but also that they have a vital role to play in calling the world to justice. Perhaps the heart of Mother Teresa's understanding was the realisation that her work was not an achievement but simply something done for its own sake, something beautiful for God. She reminds us that there is nothing as near as the eternal. The life and passion of a person leaves an imprint on the ether of a place. Mother Teresa left quite an imprint. We need people to fire our imaginative lives with a vision of life's possibilities. Mother Teresa showed us the way of passionate intensity.

She had no fear of death, as it has been with her since birth and was only the completion of her life's cycle. By releasing herself from the earth of death, which is the root of all our fears, she freed herself to live her life more fully. Like the fourteenth-century mystic Meister Eckhart before her, she believed that outside God there is nothing but nothing.

Mother Teresa's death in 1997 saddened the world. The Indian government gave her a state funeral, where the country observed a national day of mourning. Her last action was to lift her hand and touch and kiss the crucifix. Her final words were to offer her sufferings along with those of Jesus, all the while whispering, 'Jesus, I love you. Jesus, I offer myself to you. My God, I thank you, praise you and adore you. Jesus, I love you.'

Mother Teresa's death was an experience shared throughout the world. Within minutes our television sets brought the sad reality into our homes with disturbing immediacy. The images broadcast on televisions throughout the world ensured that the event belonged to everyone. The mourning for Mother Teresa was, like the mourning for Princess Diana, a communal experience.

Her followers united to grieve in a safe and private place, even amid millions of other viewers, to grapple with the sadness that enveloped them.

The noise of clapped out, spluttering engines was relentless as cars and buses packed the streets. There was not an inch of pavement in view through the mass of people, some walking, some begging, some just lying down on the path asleep. Old and frail Hindu women knelt on the streets, praying in front of cardboard boxes covered with satin and bedecked with incense sticks and little night lights shining in front of pictures of Mother Teresa.

The funeral altar was set on a rostrum covered in the blue and white colours of Mother Teresa's Missionaries of

Charity. Lotus blossoms were pinned all around the edges of the rostrum. The funeral began with the cortège leaving St Thomas's Church in the compound of the Provincial House of the Loreto order in Middleton Row. It passed through the streets of Calcutta, in which she had worked for so many years taking in the sick and the dying. Everywhere the cortège passed was swarmed with the people of Calcutta, who came to pay their final respects to this woman who made her home in their city, and who they knew simply as Mother.

It was poignant that one of her great admirers and champions, Princess Diana, died so tragically only a week before her. They had met and become friends in life, but that week they became joined in death. Mother Teresa paid tribute to Diana for being devoted to the poor. She said at the time of Diana's death, 'All the sisters and I are praying for her, and all the members of her family, to know God's speed and peace and comfort in this moment.'

Many people around the world were plunged into grief by the untimely and tragic death of Diana and were now grieving a second time over the passing of Mother Teresa. Some heads of state who had travelled to London for Diana's funeral found themselves together again a week later at the funeral Mass for Mother Teresa. Hilary Clinton, the Duchess of Kent, Queen Sofia of Spain, Sonia Gandhi from India, Queen Fabiola of Belgium, Madame Chirac, wife of the French president, Queen Noor of Jordan, and President Aquino of the Philippines were just some of the dignitaries present. All of these prominent women congregated to pay their final respects to a woman who devoted all of her energies to the poorest of the poor.

Mother Teresa lay in repose in front of the altar; her mortal remains covered in one of her saris. Enormous wreaths of highly scented lotus blossoms surrounded her. The archbishop of Calcutta celebrated the Mass and her fellow Missionaries of Charity sang.

There were long queues, day and night, outside St Thomas's Church while she lay in state. As the people filed past her, they prayed, cried, kissed her feet, lifted tiny children to touch her robes and left flowers by her side. There were banners, posters and billboards with messages of love for Mother Teresa all over the city. One in particular captured the mood of the event: 'We mourn for the loss of our Mother.'

There is a sign on the door of the home for the dying in Calcutta, saying: 'I am on my way to heaven.' One of the great crosses in Mother Teresa's life was the fact that, due to the situation in then communist Albania, where practicing religion could result in a prison sentence of up to ten years, she was unable to see her own mother for many years before her death. 'We will meet in heaven,' she would say. Her sisters believed that those who enter into a relationship of friendship with Jesus and love one another here on earth already possess eternal life, that heaven is the fullness of that life and that this was the destiny awaiting Mother Teresa.

The most moving tribute to this extraordinary woman though, was the tears from those who never met her but felt they knew her as a friend – a poignant, and appropriate, homage to a woman who embodied the virtue of 'not counting the cost'.

After Mother Teresa's death it emerged that her interior life, hidden even from those close to her, was marked by a deep, painful, and abiding feeling of being separated from God, even rejected by Him, along with an ever-increasing longing for His love. She called this inner experience 'the darkness'. It also became apparent that she had suffered from crippling doubts for long periods of her life. She wondered if she was doing the right thing and found it hard to see where God was in the midst of so much poverty and suffering. It came as a major shock to discover that Mother Teresa had doubts bordering on despair. It was at that moment, perhaps, that people saw her real sanctity, her true heroism. No pilgrimage is without crises.

The 'painful night' of her soul, which began around the time she started her work for the poor and continued until the end of her life – fifty years in all – led Mother Teresa to an even more profound union with God. Pope John Paul II, in reference to this aspect of Mother Teresa's, life said:

> In the darkest hours she clung even more tenaciously to prayer before the Blessed Sacrament. This harsh spiritual trial led her to identify herself more and more closely with those whom she served each day,

feeling their pain and, at times, even their rejection. She was fond of repeating that the greatest poverty is to be unwanted, to have no one to take care of you.

Let us praise the Lord for this diminutive woman in love with God, a humble Gospel messenger and a tireless benefactor of humanity. In her we honour one of the most important figures of our time. Let us welcome her message and follow her example.

Mother Teresa was one of the very few people who were canonised by popular acclaim, even before her death. Amid the dirt and the dying in Calcutta's slums, in the depths of the most appalling poverty, she revealed the face of God. She gave witness to the power of love, and its ability to light up even the darkest places. Perhaps the greatest thing she continues to do is inspire people to do good things. Mother Teresa shows us how to make the right choices, to have a heart that never hardens, a temper that never tires, and a touch that never hurts.

Pope John Paul II personally fast-tracked her beatification because 'she made those who had been defeated by life feel the tenderness of God'.

I am enthralled by the compassion of God and Jesus to people. I am always inspired by the image of Jesus in the gospels. He brought the compassion of God to people, and did not judge or condemn. He was someone who was with people wherever they were, especially those who found themselves on the margins of society. The work Mother Teresa and those like her do with people who are unable to help themselves is very admirable. The nature of goodness shines through Mother Teresa and her work: if we want to know what goodness is, we do not need to give big sermons or read heavy tomes — we just need to recall her work. That is why I was so keen to meet her.

In 1992, I wrote to Mother Teresa, more in hope than in confidence, seeking an interview with her. To my astonishment, she wrote to me and invited me to meet her when she came to Dublin to receive the Freedom of the City the following year. On 31 May 1993, she travelled to Dublin and on 1 June she addressed a crowd of approximately five thousand people at the Marian shrine in Knock.

At one stage in the interview, I asked her how she suffered personally and shared the sacrifice of Jesus on the cross.

She pointed to my tape recorder and said: 'That and all that world.' I could see that she approached dealings with the media in the same way I approached trips to the dentist. Glory and fame were anathema to her but, although disconcerted by all the fuss, she saw it as an opportunity to further spread the message about the poor.

The enduring memory of meeting Mother Teresa for the first time is of an incredibly energetic woman, with a radiant smile and a warm voice, who was totally fulfilled in all aspects of her life. Listening to her talk, it was difficult to imagine her giving in to despair or doubting the power of God in her life, even though pain was the background music of her life for so long. Her faith was clearly a consolation and it animated her every waking moment. Sometimes her faith appeared almost childlike. It was a rock-solid, devout faith. Her certainty could only be envied.

I have to confess, I did feel a strong pang of jealousy when I met Mother Teresa. Her God was different to mine. She had stumbled on a God who dances and astonishes. Her love of God had transported her, shattered her and consumed her like a fire. Hers was a passionate, heart-battering God, a God who swept her up to the heights in a blaze of flame, whose face was full of the beauty of all creatures, a God of incredible power and glory. Such was the beauty of this God that we can only partially taste its essence.

Mother Teresa was like a shaft of light illuminating the monstrous barbarism of poverty and injustice around her – a noble nature standing up for the people she served and loved. Preserving that cherished legacy remains important for those who saw it at first hand.

My interview with Mother Teresa covered many topics, including her thoughts on Advent and Christmas. This book deals with her reflections on these two major feasts in the Church's year.

Mother Teresa believed profoundly that the child born in a stable in Bethlehem for whom 'there was no room in the inn' still has the power to challenge contemporary society in a very powerful way. One of the most important truths of the Christian faith that Christmas embodies is the fact of God's trust in humanity. The Nativity highlights most starkly the full measure of human responsibility and human destiny as it is a declaration of God's trust in humankind. The unknown God, who is lord of all, discloses to people that if they want to know what he is like, they should look in the stable – at a human life.

Noted Jewish philosopher Emmanuel Levinas has argued persuasively that God created people because he wanted someone to speak with. This was why his word had to be made flesh. This insight reminds us that God is a living God, someone who loves people and loves to be loved by people.

Mother Teresa believed that the baby came as 'the way, the truth, and the life'. He came to bring the good news to the poor. It was a particular kind of good news because its truth hurts as much as it liberates. Sadly, there are many cosy corners that need to be challenged and many aspects of society that stand in need of liberation.

When I interviewed her in 1993, I probed Mother Teresa on her feelings about Advent and Christmas. For Mother Teresa herself, God often seemed distant and she went through her own 'dark night of the soul' for many years. She believed Advent should be a time for, in her own words, 'a spiritual self-examination'.

She reminds us that the best way for us to put Christ back into Christmas is by integrating the outcasts in society.

Reflections for each day of Advent

Day 1

Advent is important to me. I like to think of it as a 'spiritual self-examination'. There is a prayer written by Cardinal Newman that the Missionaries of Charity pray every day, which is particularly relevant to Advent:

> Jesus, help me to spread your fragrance wherever I am.
> Fill my heart with your Spirit and your life.
> Penetrate my being and take such hold of me that my life becomes a radiation of your own life.
> Give me your light through me and remain in me in such a way that every soul I come into contact with can feel your presence in me.
> May people not see me, but see you in me.

Mother Teresa

Remain in me, so that I shine with your light,
And may others be illuminated by my light.
All light will come from you, Oh Jesus.
Not even the smallest ray of light will be mine. You will
illuminate others through me.

Amen.

Day 2

To me, Advent is the season of the poor. Poverty has not
been created by God. We are the ones who have created
poverty. Before God, we are all poor. Jesus is the one we
take care of, visit, clothe, feed, and comfort every time we
do any of these for the poorest of the poor, the sick, the
dying, the lepers, and the ones who suffer from AIDS.
Should we not serve the poor like they were Jesus, we have
refused to be instruments of love in the hands of God, to
give the poor a piece of bread, to offer them a dress with
which to ward off the cold: this has happened because we
did not recognise Christ when, once more, He appeared
under the guise of pain, identified with a man numb

from the cold, dying of hunger, when He came in a lonely human being, in a lost child in search of a home.
God can work through nothings – small things like us.
He uses us to do His work.

Day 3

In the slums, I see Christ in the distressing disguise of the poor — in the broken bodies, in the children, in the dying. That is why his work becomes possible. I honestly believe that God is much closer to us than I ever would have thought possible.

We should serve the poor because they are Jesus.

The poor, anywhere in the world, are Christ who suffers.

In them, the Son of God lives and dies.

Through them, God shows his face.

Day 4

Not a day goes by without something extraordinary happening. Always in our work we are motivated by the thought: 'There, but for the grace of God, go we.'

To be happy with God on earth presupposes certain things: to love the way he loves; to help the way he helps; to give the way he gives; to save the way he saves; to remain in his presence twenty-four hours a day; to touch him in the poor and in those who suffer.

When we touch the sick and needy, we touch the suffering of Christ.

I pay no attention to numbers; what matters is the people. I rely on one. There is only one: Jesus.

Day 5

We must have endurance. What does Jesus utter on the cross? My God, my God, why hast Thou forsaken me? We shall labour in vain if God Himself does not come to our assistance.

The Apostle says: 'I can do all things in Him who sustains and comforts me.'

We must begin with faith. It is essential to have the virtues firmly imprinted on our heart.

Our first thoughts should be of God.

The grace of Jesus Christ Our Lord be with you forever.

Day 6

I am just a pencil in the hands of the Lord. It is His work. We are called upon not to be successful but to be faithful. Holinesss is for everyone. It is not for the special few but the simple duty of all. I have nothing myself.

I think God is wanting to show His greatness by using nothingness. When I speak, I speak in the name of Christ. Without Him I could do nothing.

There is a sort of miracle every day. There is not a day without some delicate attention of God, some sign of His love and care; like the time we ran out of food because of rains and flood. At the same time, the schools closed in Calcutta and all the bread was given to us so that the people would not go hungry. For two days, our poor had bread, until they could eat no more.

Day 7

We need to find God in Advent, and He cannot be found in noise.

God is the friend of silence. See how nature grows in silence; see the stars, the moon and sun, how they move in silence.

Is not our mission to give God to the poor? Not a dead God, but a living, loving God. We need silence to be able to touch souls.

The essential thing is not what we say, but what God says to us and through us.

Place on my lips your greatest praise,
Illuminating others around me.
May I preach you with actions more than with words,

with the example of my actions, with the visible light of the love that comes from you to my heart.

Amen.

Day 8

It was St Vincent de Paul who used to say to those who wanted to join his congregation: 'Never forget, my children, that the poor are our masters. That is why we should love them and serve them, with utter respect, and do what they bid us.' We treat the poor like they are a garbage bag in which we throw everything we have no other use for. Food we do not like or that is going bad — we throw it there. This does not show any respect for the dignity of the poor; this is not to consider them our masters, like St Vincent de Paul taught his religious, but to consider them less than our equals. That message still needs to be learned in the West today as well.

Day 9

They know what I mean when I talk of doing little things with great love, and that my message is simple even though it is not easy. Jesus wanted to help by sharing our life, our loneliness, our agony, our death. Only by being one with us has He redeemed us.

We are allowed to do the same: all the desolation of the poor people, not only their material poverty, but their spiritual destitution, must be redeemed. We must share the destitution, for only by being one with them can we redeem them, by bringing God into their lives and bringing them to God.

Day 10

Without our suffering our work would just be social work.
If you accept suffering and offer it to God; those who
accept it willingly, those who love deeply, those who offer
themselves, know its value.

A Hindu man came to our home for the dying at a time
when I was busy curing the wounds of a sick person. He
watched me for a while in silence. Then he said, 'Since it
gives you the strength to do what you do, I have no doubt
that your religion has to be true.'

What person have I admired most in my lifetime? One of
them was Oscar Romero, the archbishop of San Salvador.
Only minutes before a bullet from an assassin's rifle tore
through his chest, Oscar Romero preached on the gospel

he had just read: 'Whoever, out of love of Christ, gives himself to the service of others, will live like the grain of wheat that dies and only apparently dies. If it did not die, it would remain alone. Only in giving ourselves totally, can we produce a harvest.'

Day 11

What is my advice to people for Advent? My advice to the people is love to pray. Prayer enlarges the heart until it is capable of containing God's gift of himself. Ask and seek, and your heart will grow big enough to receive him as your own.

I don't want the work to become a business. It must remain a work of love. Money: I never give it a thought. It always comes. I do not want money in the bank. I need money to use for my people. We do all our work for our Lord. He must look after us. If He wants something done, He must provide us with the means. If He does not provide us with the means, then it shows that He does not want that particular work. I forget about it. It is better to serve than be served. This is His work, not mine. As long as we remain wedded to Him and our poverty, the work will prosper. I am not important. If people criticise me — so be it.

Day 12

Prayer is a recurring word in my vocabulary at Advent.
Prayer feeds the soul. As blood is to the body, prayer is to
the soul. Prayer brings you closer to God.

We want the poor to be loved and feel loved. We cannot go
to them with sad faces. God loves a cheerful giver. He
gives most who gives with joy. Joy is prayer; joy is
strength. Joy is love. Joy is a net of love by which you can
catch souls. The best way to show your gratitude to God
and the people is to accept everything with joy. A joyful
heart is the normal result of a heart burning with love.
Never let anything so fill you with sorrow as to make you
forget the joy of Christ risen.

Day 13

Am I ever afraid? No. I have given my life to God. Once we were going to go to Sudan with food. There was a danger of shooting. Five of us signed a document that we were ready to die if the plane was shot down. The next day, when we were to leave, there was a threat to shoot down the plane. The pilot refused to go. Otherwise we would have certainly gone. I believe in hope. Advent is a time of hope.

Am I frustrated? No, never. Sometimes, I am sad. A woman came to us in Calcutta with a sick baby in her arms. We were going to do our best, and she gave me the little one. But the baby died right there in my arms. I saw that woman's face as she stood there, and I felt the way she did.

Why do we need hope? It is hope that sustains us. What
we hope for is what He promised: a new heaven and a new
earth. Jesus came to bring 'the good news to the poor'.
The glow of God's love is always available.

I have a happiness that no one can take from me. There
has never been a doubt or any unhappiness. I do get
angry sometimes; when I see waste, when the things that
are wasted are what people need, things that could save
them from dying.

Day 14

Some of my sisters work in Australia. On a
reservation, among the Aborigines, there was an
elderly man. I can assure you that you have never seen
a situation as difficult as that poor old man's. He was
completely ignored by everyone. His home was
disordered and dirty.

I told him, 'Please, let me clean your house, wash your
clothes, and make your bed.'

He answered, 'I'm okay like this. Let it be.'

I said again, 'You will be still better if you allow me to
do it.'

He finally agreed. So I was able to clean his house and
wash his clothes. I discovered a beautiful lamp,
covered with dust. Only God knows how many years
since he last lit it.

I said to him, 'Don't you light your lamp? Don't you ever use it?'

He answered, 'No. No one comes to see me. I have no need to light it. Who would I light it for?'

I asked, 'Would you light it every night if the sisters came?'

He replied, 'Of course.'

From that day on the sisters committed themselves to visiting him every evening. We cleaned the lamp, and the sisters would light it every evening.

Two years passed. I had completely forgotten that man. He sent this message: 'Tell my friend that the light she lit in my life continues to shine still.'

Day 15

I chose to call a form of newsletter I write for our
sisters *Ek Dil*, a Hindi term, an expression describing
the unity among the sisters in their houses all over
the globe. *Ek Dil* means 'one heart'.

There are so many religions and each one has its
different ways of following God. I follow Christ: Jesus
is my God. There is only one God and He is God to all;
therefore it is important that everyone is seen as
equal before God. I've always said we should help a
Hindu become a better Hindu, a Muslim become a
better Muslim, a Catholic become a better Catholic.
Advent calls me to be a better Catholic.

Day 16

Our Lord wanted me to be a free nun, covered with the poverty of the cross. But I learned a great lesson after I left the Loreto. When looking for a home I walked and walked until my legs and arms ached. I thought how much others must ache in soul and body looking for a home, food and health. Then the comfort of Loreto came to tempt me, but of my own free choice, my God, and out of love for you, I desire to remain and do whatever be your holy will in my regard.

One of my clearest memories of our work in Calcutta is that late in the day, around ten at night, when the doorbell rang. I opened the door and found a man shivering from the cold. 'Mother Teresa, I heard that you just received an important prize. When I heard this I decided to offer you something too. Here you have it: this is what I collected today.' It was little, but in his case it was everything. I was more moved by what he did than by the Nobel Prize.

Day 17

Do I believe in the God of small things? Look what
God is doing with nothing. People must believe that it
is all His, all His. We must allow God to use us,
without adding or subtracting anything.

Side by side with their spiritual training, our sisters have
to go to the slums. Slum work and this meeting with the
people is part of their training so that we all give our
wholehearted free service to the poorest of the poor – to
Christ in his distressing disguise. Because of this it is
necessary that they come face to face with the reality, so
as to be able to understand what their life is going to be
when they have taken their vows, when they will have to
meet Christ twenty-four hours a day in the poorest of the
poor in the slums or on the streets.

Day 18

Am I at peace? I have to work hard for inner peace —
when I seek solitude, silence and waiting, to be with
God. I have interior trials and feelings of dryness, but
my soul lives with a remembrance and tender love of
our Lord. I only know that God will give me the grace
to find, in His way, my peace of mind. Advent is a
time of reaching out to the Prince of Peace.

Peace I leave you.

My peace I give you.

Let each of us make the sign of peace daily.

Day 19

God was born as a baby to highlight that in our weakness we will find strength to live the Christian life. If we were strong enough to do everything ourselves we would not have needed Jesus in the first place.

Thomas Merton wrote: 'With those for whom there is no room, Christ is present in this world.'

I like to think also that, especially at Advent and Christmas, with those for whom there is no one to share their rooms is Jesus. The sad reality is that life is difficult for many people. The message of Advent and Christmas is that Christ is made flesh not in the unreal beauty of the Christmas card, but in the poor of our world. For those of us who claim to be Christian, Christ is made flesh in the poor.

Day 20

We are Missionaries of Charity, and a missionary is a person who has to go and spread the good news. It makes no difference, today in India, tomorrow in Ireland, anywhere the voice of God calls you. Missionaries are people who are sent to become a carrier of God's love. That's why we are called Missionaries of Charity. Someone once said to me: 'You are spoiling the poor by giving everything to them.' Then I said, 'Nobody has spoiled us more than God Himself.' He is also giving. He is total giving. Another person said to me: 'Why do you give them a fish to eat? Why don't you give them a rod to catch the fish?' So I replied, 'My people, when I pick them up, they can't even stand. They are either sick or hungry. So I take them.' Once they are all right, they don't come to me anymore, for they can stand on their own.

For Advent, we are all called to be Missionaries of God's love.

Day 21

A beautiful thing happened in Calcutta. Two young people came to see me, Hindu people. They gave me a very big amount of money. 'How did you get so much money?' I asked them. They answered me, 'We got married two days ago. Before our marriage, we decided we would not have a big wedding feast and we would not buy wedding clothes. We decided that we would give the money we saved to you to feed the people.' In a rich Hindu family, it is a scandal not to have special wedding clothes and not to have a wedding feast. 'Why did you do that?' I asked them. They answered me, 'Mother, we love each other so much that we wanted to obtain a special blessing from God by making a sacrifice. We wanted to give each other this special gift.' Is that not beautiful?

Things like that are happening every day, really beautiful things. We must pull them out. We have to pull out the wonderful things that are happening as well as the bad things.

Day 22

A Hindu man was once asked: 'What is a Christian?'
He responded, 'The Christian is someone who gives.'
Give until it hurts, until you feel the pain. Open your
hearts to the love God instills in them. God loves you
tenderly. What he gives you is not to be kept under
lock and key, but to be shared. The more you have, the
less you will be able to give. The less you have, the
more you will know how to share. Let us ask God,
when it comes time to ask him for something, to help
us to be generous.

Day 23
One of my sisters once read a passage to me:

Go with the people
Live with them
Learn from them
Love them
Start with what they know
Build with what they have
But with the best leaders
When the work is done
The task accomplished
The people will say
'We have done this ourselves.'
(Lao Tzu)

Day 24

Our works of love are nothing but works of peace. Let us
do them with greater love and efficiency. Let us radiate
the peace of God and so light and extinguish in the world
and in the hearts of all people all hatred, and love for
power. If you really love that person, then it will be easier
for you to accept that person and it will be with love and
kindness. For that is an opportunity for you to put your
love for God in living action.

How do I react to violence in the world? Let us not use
bombs and guns to overcome the world. Let us use
love and compassion. Let us preach the peace of
Christ as He did. He went about doing good. If
everyone could see the image of God in his neighbour,
do you think we would need tanks and generals?

Day 25

When I visited China in 1969, one of the Communist party asked me: 'Mother Teresa what is a communist to you?' I answered, 'A child of God, a brother, a sister of mine.' 'Well, you think highly of us. But where did you get that idea?' I told him, 'From God Himself. He said, truly I tell you, just as you did it to one of the least of these who are members of my family, you did it to me.'

Peace and war begin at home. If we truly want peace in the world, let us begin by loving one another in our own families. If we want to spread joy, we need for every family to have joy. God has created us so we do small things with great love. I believe in that great love that comes, or should come, from our heart should start at home: with my family, my neighbours across the secret, those right next door. And this love should then reach everyone.

Day 26

I once picked up a woman from a garbage dump and she was burning with fever: she was in her last days and her only lament was: 'My son did this to me.' I begged her to forgive her son. I told her that in a moment of madness when he was not himself, he did something he would regret. I asked her to be a mother to him and forgive him. It took me a long time to make her say: 'I forgive my son.' Just before she died, she was able to say that with real forgiveness.

At Advent we must forgive.
We must become channels of forgiveness.
Make us instruments of God's forgiveness.
Make us instruments of God's peace.

Day 27

A young man was dying in one of our homes, but for three or four days fought to prolong his life. The sister there asked him: 'Why do you continue this fight?' He answered: 'I cannot die without asking forgiveness from my father.'

When his father arrived, the youth embraced him and asked forgiveness. Two hours later, the young man passed away peacefully.

Forgive those who have hurt you, this Advent.

Make peace with those who have wounded you, this Christmas.

Be a missionary for forgiveness.

Be a missionary for peace.

Day 28

Gandhi said he was impressed by your Christ but not
your Christians. If people were as good at living
Christianity as they were at talking about it there would
be no need for our work here.

St Francis of Assisi wrote:

> Let the whole of humanity tremble ...
> That the Lord of the universe,
> God and the Son of God,
> so humbles Himself
> that for our salvation
> He hides Himself under the little form of bread!

Let us find Jesus this Advent.
Let us seek Jesus at the Lord's table this Christmas.

Day 29

I never forget what happened to our sisters in Rome, where we work with the shut-ins. They go to the poor people's houses. We clean the house and give them a bath, wash their clothes in the house and so on. The sisters found someone left in terrible condition. They cleaned his room and washed his clothes and gave him a good bath, but he never spoke.

After two days he told his sisters, 'You have brought God into my life, bring father also.'

This Advent may we find God the Father.

This Advent may we find God the Son.

This Advent may we find God the Spirit.

May our love shine in every house.

May our love shine for those with no house.

Day 30

I look forward to Christmas. What we celebrate at this time of the year is a simple but profound truth: God so loved the world that he sent us the greatest gift of all: His only son to save us. Other religions speak of the divination of man. We celebrate the humanisation of God. The birth of a baby put a smile on the face of the world. This baby comes with a call to all of us to serve. If one gives a little bit of rice to a poor person in India, the person feels satisfied and happy. The poor in the West do not accept their poverty, and for many it is a source of despair. This season we can be a bridge between those who have and those who have less.

Reflection for the Feast of the
Immaculate Conception

One of my favourite prayers is: Mary, Mother of Jesus, give me your heart, so beautiful, so pure, so immaculate, so full of love and humility that I may be able to receive Jesus in the Bread of Life, love Him as you loved Him and serve Him in the Poorest of the Poor.

In 1984, the Holy Father was celebrating Mass outside in St Peter's Square, and there was a great crowd. A group of Missionaries of Charity were also there. Suddenly it started to rain. I told the sisters, 'Let us pray a quick novena of *Memorare* to Our Lady so it stops raining.' While we were praying the second *Memorare*, it started to rain even harder. While we prayed the third, the fourth, the fifth, the sixth, the seventh, and the eighth ones, the umbrellas started to close. By the time we finished the ninth prayer, the only open umbrellas were ours; we had worried so much about praying that we had not paid attention to the weather. It had stopped raining.

Reflections for each Day of Christmas

Day 1
Who is Jesus for me?
He is:
The Word made flesh.
The Bread of life.
The Way to be Walked.
The Joy to be shared.
The Peace to be given.
The Leper — to wash his wounds.
The Beggar — to give him a smile.
The Drunkard — to listen to him.
The Mentally ill — to protect him.
The Little one — to embrace him.
The Blind — to lead him.

The Dumb – to speak for him.
The Crippled – to walk with him.
The drug addict – to befriend him.
The Prostitute – to remove from danger and befriend.
The Prisoner – to be visited.
The Old – to be served.

Day 2

One of our novices had just entered the Congregation after finishing her studies at the university. Before she and another sister left to care for the poor one day, 1 reminded them, 'You know where you have to go. During the Mass, notice how tenderly and lovingly the priest touches the Body of Christ. Do not forget, that Christ is the same Christ you touch in the poor.' The two sisters left. One of them, the novice, knocked on my door. She told me, full of joy, 'Mother, 1 touched the Body of Christ for the last three hours.' Her face reflected her deep joy. 'What did you do?' 1 asked her.

'Right after we arrived,' she answered, 'they brought us a man covered with wounds. He had been picked up from

the rubble. I had to help take care of his wounds. It took
three hours. Therefore, I touched the Body of Christ for
three hours. I am sure it was Him.'
At Christmas, we reach Jesus in the Eucharist.
Let us pray together at the table of the Lord.

Day 3

What is the greatest lesson life has taught me? In this life
we cannot do great things, we can only do small things
with great love. I am more convinced of the work being
His than I am convinced I am really alive.

The message of Christmas is the same as every other day,
though:

> For I was a stranger and you gave me welcome,
> I was naked and you gave me clothes,
> I was hungry and thirsty and you gave me food and
> drink,
> I was in pain and you gave me comfort.
> We must be like Jesus.
> We must find Jesus in others every day.
> We must bring Jesus to others.

Day 4

I suppose my greatest wish to everyone at this special time
is summed up in the words of the Celtic Blessing:

> Our God, God of all men,
> God of heaven and earth, sea and rivers,
> God of sun and moon, of all the stars,
> God of high mountains and of lowly valleys,
> God over heaven, and in heaven, and under heaven.
> He has a dwelling in heaven and earth and sea
> and in all things that are in them.
> He breathes in all things, makes all things live,
> supports all things ...
> He lights the sun, makes wells ...
> Deep peace of the running waves to you,
> Deep peace of the shining stars to you
> Deep peace of the Prince of Peace to you.

Day 5

Christmas is an ideal time to be reborn in Christ.
Jesus became a child to teach us to love God. In the
eyes of the child, I see the spirit of life, of God. What
we say does not matter, only what God says through
us. The poor call to us. We have to be aware of them
in order to love them. We have to ask ourselves if we
know the truth. Those who work with me know this. If
there were poor on the moon, they would go there too.
They know that the poor are precisely the ones who
better understand human dignity. If they have a
problem, it is not lack of money, but the fact that
their right to be treated humanly, and with
tenderness, is not recognised.

Good works are like links that form a chain of love.

Day 6

The heart of God's invitation to us at Christmas is love because through love alone we please God, and our main challenge is to acquire it. Jesus came on earth to love and be loved – to win love for our love. The Christian life is an exchange of love – the love we receive and the love we give God.

That is not as easy as it sounds. As we read (in the second letter of Timothy), there's the soldier who in war must be disciplined, obedient and courageous; the farmer who toils long hours and never has the luxury of a day off, and the athlete who pushes his body to the limit to maintain peak fitness and whose sights are fixed exclusively on winning the race. We must love until it hurts.

Day 7

I have a favourite Christmas story from our world today.
It is the story of how Christmas stopped a war when the
fierce and bloody First World War came to a halt on the
day of Christ's birth in one corner of the Western Front.
The Germans waved and called out speaking in simple
French, holding out cigars they asked for English jam in
return. 'Stille Nacht' and 'Silent Night' rang out on
different sides. The words were different but the
sentiments remained the same. A football was produced
and a game took place. It is a lovely story of peace.
What would my Christmas Blessing be for the world?
Somebody once gave me a blessing:

This Christmas may you have
Joy enough to share with the world,

Mother Teresa

Peace enough to calm the world
Love enough to light the world.

Day 8

When our sisters come to me they do so in a spirit of sacrifice. Once a group of teachers from the United States came to visit me in Calcutta. Before they left, one of them asked me if I would say something that they could keep as a remembrance of the visit and that would also be useful to them. I answered: 'Smile at one another. Smile at your wives.' One of them said, 'Mother, it is obvious that you are not married!'

'Yes I am,' I answered. 'Sometimes it is very difficult for me to smile at Jesus because he asks too much of me.'

Even when it is difficult for them, our sisters come with a smile.

Christmas is a time to smile.

Let us bring a smile to others this Christmas.

Mother Teresa

Let us bring the smile of Jesus to others.
Let us give a smile to those too damaged to smile.

Day 9

I like poetry. One Christmas a Carmelite priest gave me a copy of St John of the Cross's poem 'The Incarnation' which reads:

> Then He called
> The archangel Gabriel
> And sent him to
> The Virgin Mary,
> At whose consent
> The mystery was wrought,
> In whom the Trinity
> Clothed the Word with flesh,
> And though three work this,
> It is wrought in the one;
> And the Word lived incarnate
> In the tomb of Mary.

Mother Teresa

And He who had only a father
Now had a Mother too,
But she was not like others
Who conceive by man.
From her own flesh
He received His flesh
So he is called
Son of God and of man.

Day 10
I speak of God at times at Christmas almost like a love affair.
St John of the Cross put it beautifully:

> My beloved is the mountains,
> and lonely wooded valleys,
> strange islands
> and resounding rivers,
> The whistling of love-stirring breezes

> The tranquil night
> at the time of rising dawn,
> Silent music,
> sounding solitude,
> The supper that refreshes, and deepens love.

> Jesus is my everything.

Day 11

That love of God directs us in a particular way.

It is God's will that all people should be saved in Christ.

When we pray the Stations of the Cross we say:

> O Jesus for love of me didst bear thy cross to Calvary
> In thy sweet mercy grant me to suffer and to die with thee.

But we also pray especially at Christmas:

> Thou O Lord wilt open my lips.
> And my tongue shall announce Thy praise.

At Christmas we sing praise for all that God has given us.

Day 12

My understanding of Christ and Christmas is clearly forged on the basis of my own relationship with Him. Without Him, we could do nothing. It is at the altar that we meet our suffering poor. In Him, we see that suffering can become a means to greater love, and greater generosity.

To me, Jesus is my God.
Jesus is my Spouse.
Jesus is my Life.
Jesus is my only Love.
Jesus is my all in all.

Beautiful faces are they that wear
the light of a pleasant spirit there.

Beautiful hands are they that do,
deeds that are noble, good and true;
Beautiful feet are they that go,
swiftly to lighten another's woe.

Afterword

Blessed Art Thou Amongst Women:
Mother Teresa's Story

When Mother Teresa died, she left behind two saris and a bucket, the sum total of her worldly possessions. She became Blessed Teresa of Calcutta because she identified herself with the Person of Jesus who she encountered every day in her prayer life, in the Eucharist and in the service of the poorest of the poor.

These are some of the crucial dates in her life and also some context to help understand their significance:

26 August 1910: Mother Teresa was born Agnes Gonxha Bojaxhiu in Skopje, Albania, now part of the Republic of Macedonia.

26 September 1928: Agnes left for Zagreb by train to travel to the Loreto Abbey in Rathfarnham in Dublin. It was the last time she ever saw her mother.

The Loreto sisters had a long connection with India. Their founder, Mary Ward was born near York in 1585, and predicted the apostolic influence of women in times to come in families, in public life, and in the Church. At age 15 she was called into religious life. She went to enter a Poor Clare convent. Through special insights, God revealed to her when she was 24 that 'some other thing' was destined for her and that she had a special calling. She went on to pioneer a new type of religious life for women in the creation of Catholic schools for girls. After she left the Poor Clares, Mary Ward worked in disguise to preserve the Catholic faith in England before founding a community of active sisters in 1609 in Northern France. Unlike the cloistered sisters in other convents, she and her companions educated young women, helped persecuted and imprisoned Catholics, and spread the

word of God in places priests could not go. The sisters
lived and worked openly on the continent, but in England
they had to work secretly.

Some of Mary Ward's ideas about religious life were
viewed with suspicion because they were so revolutionary
at the time. She developed three essential requirements
for her institute. The first, and most critical, was not to be
enclosed. Next she sought government by a woman as
general superior, which bordered on heresy at the time.
Finally she required flexibility in the hours of prayer. She
was anxious that her sisters would not face tension
between attending prayers at set times and tending to
those in need. Mary was imprisoned by Church officials
who called her a dangerous heretic for her efforts to
expand the religious in spreading the faith. In 1630, while
she was imprisoned in a convent in Munich, Pope Urban

VIII compared her institution to 'a weed in the cornfield'. Her work was destroyed and her sisters scattered. But she never lost hope, and kept the flame burning. When Mary Ward died in 1645 her sisters were still suffering from a tainted reputation. Only in 1713 did Pope Benedict XIII agree to recognise the institute, as long as it airbrushed out Mary Ward's name as founder. By 1953 though, the Vatican would describe her as 'this incomparable young woman whom England gave to the Church'.

The founder of the Irish Branch of the institute of the Blessed Virgin Mary was Frances Ball. She was born in Dublin on 9 January 1794. At the age of 9 she was sent to school at the Bar Convent, York, Institute of the Blessed Virgin Mary. In 1814, Frances Ball was received into the Bar Convent Novitiate at the request of Dr Daniel Murray, the archbishop of Dublin, to be trained as religious of the

Institute of the Blessed Virgin Mary with the view to establishing a foundation in Ireland. There she received her religious training and made her profession in 1816, taking the name of Mary Teresa. In 1821, at the request of Dr Murray she returned to Dublin with two novices to establish a convent and school there.

In 1822 she opened the first house of the Institute in Ireland, in Rathfarnham House in Dublin. As there were only three sisters there, Teresa decided to call the house 'Loreto' after the village in Italy where the Holy Family's house was said to have been miraculously transported to. The name 'Loreto House' was to be used for all the subsequent foundations that came from Ireland and resulted in the sisters of the Irish Branch of the IBVM being popularly as 'Loreto sisters'. These sisters worked with oppressed, outcast and marginalised social groups.

In 1834, such was the state of the Catholic Church in
Calcutta and Bengal that a group of Jesuits, including
priests from Ireland and elsewhere, decided to take
pastoral care of the area. This led to the opening of St
Xavier's School, which quickly attracted Muslim and
Hindu boys, as well as Christians. Its presence
highlighted the need for a comparable school for girls.
A German priest, in Dublin in 1841, urged the Loreto
sisters to send a group of missionary sisters to serve as
teachers and tend to the welfare of the needy in Calcutta.
Mother Teresa Ball met the priest, but refused his request
on the basis that the needs of the poor in Ireland had
priority. However, the priest would not take no for an
answer and indulged in moral blackmail, telling Mother
Teresa Ball that she might be responsible for the souls of
the children she was denying a Christian education.

Moved by his plea, Mother Teresa Ball allowed the priest to make his appeal directly to her community of sisters. The community was keen on the project and, as a result, seven nuns and six postulants were chosen for the mission. On 23 August 1841, they left Ireland aboard the *Scotia* and did not arrive on Indian shores until 30 December that year. The local bishop, Bishop Carew from Ireland, celebrated a Mass in their honour in the Cathedral of Our Lady of the Rosary in Calcutta. Just over a century later Mother Teresa would make her profession as a Missionary of Charity in the same cathedral.

The baker's dozen of young Irish women set up home at 5 Middleton Row and named it Loreto House. On 10 January 1842, the Loreto sisters opened their school. Such were the glowing reports from Calcutta that there was a constant supply of volunteers from Rathfarnham to India, despite forty-two young Loreto Sisters coming to premature deaths over the next twenty years. Many of the sisters did show the cumulative results of scarce resources, inadequate diet and demanding work schedules, including seven days a week rosters. However, their contribution has been enormous. George Eliot's comment on Dorothea Brooke in *Middlemarch* could apply to many of these Irish sisters in India and beyond: 'But the effect of her being on those around her was incalculably diffusive: for the growing good of the world is partly dependent on unhistoric acts; and that things are not so ill with you and me as they might have been, is half owing to the number who lived faithfully a hidden life, and rest in unvisited tombs.'

In the nineteenth century, the Catholic Church was an important agent of social change, establishing schools, hospitals, asylums, and temperance agencies for the purpose of 'evangelising and civilising the poor'. Throughout this period, Irish women entered convents in great numbers. Traditionally, the life of the woman religious was one of contemplation and the cloister. This changed with the Counter-Reformation when congregations of women religious were established to participate in more active works of charity, chiefly in teaching and nursing. With the formation of the Daughters of Charity by St Vincent de Paul in 1633, a trail was blazed for subsequent orders of women religious dedicated to the active apostolate.

Historical marginalisation was the fate of these women. These nuns were remarkable women, doing remarkable work in a difficult time. The tragedy is that their stories have never been told. So many heroic women's stories are woven almost anonymously in the tapestry of history, even though they deserve individual recognition. Most Irish nuns fit into this broader pattern.

November 1928: Mother Teresa left Ireland with Betine Kanjc for the boat to Calcutta. On the boat, they befriended three young Franciscan sisters. On the way, they went through the Suez Canal, the Red Sea, and the Indian Ocean before arriving in the Bay of Bengal and landing on January 6, 1929 in Calcutta.

24 May 1931: When Agnes Gonxha took her first vows, she took the name of Teresa to avoid confusion with a Sister Thérèse Breen, already a novice in the community.

14 May 1937: Sister Teresa took lifetime vows of poverty, chastity, and obedience as a Loreto Sister in Darjeeling. For nineteen years, Sister Teresa lived the life of a Loreto nun.

In the 1930s and 1940s, poverty was endemic in Calcutta. As the political situation in India worsened in the run-up to its independence, violence was common. Given her position as a teacher, Mother Teresa was shielded from much of the problem but she was determined to see the problems for herself.

Godfrey Moorehouse wrote, 'Its is the easiest thing in the world to come close to despair in Calcutta.' He continues, 'Every statistic that you tear out of the place reeks of doom. Every half mile can produce something that is guaranteed to turn a newcomer's stomach with fear or disgust or a sense of hopelessness.' That was not Mother

Teresa's response. Instead of turning away in despair, she was driven by her experience of the misery around her to devote her life to the service of the poorest of the poor.

10 September 1946: Mother Teresa was travelling by train from Calcutta to Darjeeling, in the foothills of the Himalayas. Suddenly, she had the inspiration to found a new order and devote herself to the poor.

8 August 1948: Mother Teresa began her mission with nothing. She identified with the poor in everything, with those whom the world seemed to reject and ignore, in her own words, with 'the unwanted, the unloved, the uncared for'. If Mother Teresa was to work among the poor, with the poor, and for the poor, then, she thought, she better wear the dress of the poor. So she dressed herself in the

simple white sari with a blue border, the dress worn by women working as scavengers in Calcutta. She would give this new religious habit a new symbol and meaning: for her the white sari came to represent holiness, and the blue border stood for our Holy Mother, Mary. Just as Bengal's women kept the keys of their houses well tied up on one end of their sari, so Mother Teresa tied a small crucifix to one end of her sari, the key to her home in heaven.

Mother Teresa was offered a place of her own by Michael Gomes, an Indian Catholic, in 14 Creek Lane in Calcutta. He refused to take any money from Mother Teresa because he was an active member of the Legion of Mary, founded in Dublin by Frank Duff. For Gomes, Mother Teresa was a blessing from God. He described her presence, saying, 'We received. We did not give.'

1949: Mother Teresa applied for, and was granted, Indian citizenship.

1971: Mother Teresa is the very first person to be nominated for the John XXIII Peace Prize. One journalist wrote about the event: 'Other people said great things about poverty. To take one example President Dwight D. Eisenhower once said: "Every gun that is made, every warship launched, every rocket fired, signifies, in the final sense, a theft from those who hunger and are not fed, those who are cold and are not clothed. This world in arms is not spending money alone. It is spending the sweat of its labourers, the genius of its scientists, the hopes of its children." Mother Teresa never said fine words like that but she did not need to because she spoke louder and more effectively by her actions.'

Although the newspapers in the late 1960s were full of Vietnam, Martin Luther King and the civil rights struggle in America, the civil war in Biafra, and the ferment in the Middle East after the Lightning War between Israel and her three Arab neighbours, Egypt, Jordan, and Syria, Mother Teresa was keenly aware of the escalating sectarian tension which preceded the civil rights demonstrations in Northern Ireland.

When the Troubles in Northern Ireland were at their height in 1971, Mother Teresa sent a group of sisters armed just with bedrolls and a violin to Belfast. They were given a tiny house whose former occupant, a priest, had been murdered. They stated their rationale for coming as: 'We have come from Calcutta to try to improve relations between the people in the whole of Belfast in whatever little way we can.'

According to reports, Mother Teresa herself once spent an hour on the phone with Ian Paisley trying to broker a peace deal but her efforts failed.

After only eighteen months though, her sisters suddenly withdrew from the province in mysterious circumstances. Speculation was rife that they did so at the request of either the local Church authorities or a specific figure within the Church itself.

When I asked her about it, Mother Teresa refused to discuss it and merely stated that it was important to always follow God's will, even when we did not understand it.

1971: Malcolm Muggeridge wrote *Something Beautiful for God*. Mother Teresa said that it should not be a biography of herself, that 'the work is God's work'.

Mother Teresa left the impression on the media as the mother who looks out for the weaker members of the families. During a TV interview with her, in one of the orphanages she founded, the presenter said, 'What a wonderful honour it is for me to meet you, Mother.' To which he got the sharp answer: 'There is no honour in that. You are honoured to be meeting these poor orphans whom nobody wants.'

1976: Mother Teresa meets the man described as 'Britain's best known Christian', Cliff Richard. When I Interviewed Sir Cliff in 1990, he told me more about the meeting:

> I met Mother Teresa just once. In 1976, I interviewed her in India for the charity Tearfund about her work with the destitute and dying. It was a powerful

experience to meet such an icon. I remember we were all very amused when we arrived at the door to her hospice, which was down a tiny alley, to find one of those old-fashioned name boards with a piece of wood which you slide from left to right to indicate whether someone is 'In' or 'Out'. There were a whole lot of names but among them we found 'Mother Teresa'. She was then in her seventies, a frail, hunched little figure.

She was awe-inspiring but also delightful. She introduced us to some of her fellow nuns — all dressed as she was — and showed us around; she showed us the holy area where they prayed, and the area where the people came in off the streets, many of them on stretchers. She was hugging the patients as we passed them, saying, 'These are sweet people, and when they die they will know that we have loved them.' That was her premise, that no one should die alone and unloved; everyone should live with dignity.

After the hour of the hospice, I interviewed her, and then — I had my guitar as usual — we all sang and then we prayed together. In the car on the way back to our hotel at the end of the day, someone said, 'Let's listen to the tape.' So we put the tape into the machine, pressed play — and nothing happened. We turned it over: nothing. We tried every inch of it: there wasn't a single syllable to be heard. As soon as we got back to the hotel I rang Mother Teresa and said, 'I'm so sorry to have to ask you this but would it be possible for us to come back?'

'Why?' she said. 'What happened?'

I said, 'There's nothing on the tape.'

Her reply was simple: 'OK, something you said or I

said must have displeased Jesus. He wiped the tape. You'd better come back. We'll do it again.' Mother Teresa could not have been more gracious and I thought: no matter how much we make people icons, a part of them has to remain real, and she was one hundred per cent real.

I came away thinking: why do we complicate our faith? Why do we have to intellectualise everything? Sometimes the intellect clouds the issue. For Mother Teresa, it was simple: one of us said something that Jesus didn't like, so come back and we'll put it right. Second time around, the recording was perfect, and it was the same tape. I would have said it was the same interview too, but maybe not.

9 December 1979: Mother Teresa arrived in Oslo to receive the Nobel Prize for Peace. One commentator observes: 'Mother Teresa is an extraordinary woman. Very many people feel a great sorrow and a great sense of loss in our world. For the abandoned and the outcasts, the little ones and the forgotten ones, she is a great sign of hope. To the poor she is a faithful and wholehearted friend.'

1980: Mother Teresa visits Berlin. There she meets the woman who will in time become her replacement as the head of her order, Sister Mary Prema. Sister Mary had been a teacher of disabled children but when she met Mother Teresa in Berlin she decided to enter the congregation. She has reflected on her memories of Mother Teresa: 'I found her to be a person full of energy and joy, who met people and shared the love of Jesus with them. She made me feel welcome and accepted and shared the common life with the sisters and always had time to listen to them. She was a kind woman. In her life, she taught me the meaning of her own comments: "Kind words can be short and easy to speak, but their echoes are truly endless."'

8 July 1981: Mother Teresa visited Corrymeela in Northern Ireland to talk about peace in a province stained by bloodshed. She quoted Pope John Paul II: 'Man cannot live without love. He remains a being that is incomprehensible for himself, his life is senseless, if love is not revealed to him, if he does not encounter love, if he does not experience it and make it his own, if he does not participate intimately in it.'

She also remarked: 'The founder of the L'Arche communities, Jean Vanier, tells us: "When the poor and weak are present, they prevent us from falling into the trap of power – even the power to good – of thinking that it is we who are the good ones."'

1984: Mother Teresa visits the devastating famine in Ethiopia. Knowing that you cannot discover new oceans unless you have the courage to lose sight of the shore, she felt she had no option but to visit the scene for herself. Having sprang to fame in the 1970s when his band the Boomtown Rats had a string of hits, most famously 'I Don't Like Mondays', Bob Geldof became a global superstar in 1984 when he devised and organised the Band Aid record 'Do They Know It's Christmas?' to alleviate the plight of the starving millions in Ethiopia.

The following year his fame increased further when he ran the phenomenally successful Live Aid concerts. In January 1985, Geldof sat in the departure lounge at Addis Ababa when he saw Mother Teresa. Photographers fell over themselves to grab pictures of this unlikely conversation – particularly given Geldof's penchant for swearing. The media had a field day with the story and dubbed them 'the saint and the sinner'. Although born into a Catholic family and educated by the Holy Ghost Fathers in Ireland's most famous rugby nursery Blackrock College, Geldof had long since renounced his Catholicism. In his 1980 hit 'Banana Republic' he had rubbished the influence of priests in Irish society.

In his 1986 autobiography *Is That It?* Geldof recalled his impressions of Mother Teresa. His first thought was how tiny she looked and that she was a 'battered, wizened woman'. Somewhat surprisingly he was then very taken by her feet. He noticed that while her habit was clean and well cared for, her sandals were simply 'beaten-up pieces of leather from which her feet protruded, gnarled and misshapen as old tree roots'. When Sir Bob bent to kiss her, as it seemed the polite thing to do, he was caught off guard when she bowed her head so quickly that he had no option but to kiss 'the top of her wimple'. Geldof admitted to being disturbed by the incident until he discovered that Mother Teresa only let lepers kiss her.

Geldof went on to tell her about when his band had played in India and offered to play a concert for her mission. She declined his offer immediately because she did not need such activities because God would provide. Geldof recalled that as the television cameras in the departure lounge were rolling, Mother Teresa grabbed the chance to say that she had observed on her way to the airport some palatial old buildings which seemed unoccupied and wanted to know if she could have them as orphanages. A government minister, brought in to the discussion, tried to kick for touch but, unable to say no on live television, he eventually conceded that he would try to find her suitable home for an orphanage. Quick as a flash, Mother Teresa said: 'Two orphanages.' Through gritted teeth he agreed: 'Two orphanages.'

Ethiopia took a hold of Mother Teresa's imagination, as it was an enduring monument to inhumanity, ineffectiveness and indifference. She linked up with the agency Ethiopiaid in Addis Ababa, Ethiopia, where a group of nuns run a compound known affectionately as the 'House of Angels'. Their constituency rank among the most desperate on earth, and nobody is turned away. The sisters run an orphanage for children who have lost their parents, many of them to HIV/AIDS. Often the children themselves are infected with HIV too, and many do not survive beyond their teens.

27 October 1986: Mother Teresa joins the great religions to pray for peace at Assisi.
In the life of Mother Teresa she gave perhaps more importance to prayer than to the actual work, but her work flowed from her prayer life. She believed that prayer puts people in touch with God and makes them capable of being His instrument. Prayer taught her to look contemplatively at the world and to see there the living presence of Jesus. The Missionaries of Charity begin their day with prayer, both personal and communal, followed by the Eucharist, which is the real centre of their

existence. Each evening they have an hour of adoration. The sisters have a rule of reciting the rosary when travelling or while walking through the streets. Everything is done in an atmosphere of prayer.

It was often said that the source and strength of Mother Teresa's whole life was the twofold commandment of love of God, and of neighbour. These two commandments cannot be separated. The fruit of faith is love. The Missionaries of Charity base their whole life on these two pillars. They take a vow of wholehearted free service to the poorest of the poor. Every morning they recite this prayer:

> Make us worthy, Lord, to serve our fellow men throughout this world who live and die in poverty and hunger. Give them, through our hands this day, their daily bread, and by our understanding love, give peace and joy.

1993: Mother Teresa comes to Ireland to receive the highest honour the Irish state could confer on her at the invitation of the then Lord Mayor of Dublin, Gay Mitchell TD and she becomes a free person of Dublin. In her life she received many honours in Ireland. In 1995 the Royal College of Surgeons in Dublin awarded her their highest award, an Honorary Fellowship of the College. She followed such illustrious winners as Nelson Mandela and former US President Jimmy Carter.

1995: The influential writer Christopher Hitchens publishes his book *The Missionary Position*, a devastating critique of Mother Teresa. He posed the question whether this 'wizened, shriveled old lady, well stricken in years' represented 'another chapter in a millennial story, which stretches back to the superstitious childhood of our species, and which depends on the exploitation of the simple and the humble by the cunning and the single-minded'.

1996: Mother Teresa marks the fiftieth anniversary of her Darjeeling experience by going to Armagh to open the 563rd house of her order. At the end of the prayers at the ceremony, helped by two of her sisters, the tiny frail 85-year-old lady struggled to her feet. As a result of an accident she had sprained her ankle and was in a wheelchair. She spoke to the audience then about prayer and love, two topics that were close to her heart.

5 September 1997: Mother Teresa died. Vincenzo Bilotta was Mother Teresa's doctor when she was in Rome and in

her later years she had many health scares, especially with her heart. Dr Bilotta has a big photo of Mother Teresa in his surgery. After she died the sisters in Calcutta rang him to tell him the news, personally. He said that her heart, which had held up for all those years, 'just gave away'.

By this year, Mother Teresa's sisters numbered nearly 4,000 members and were established in 610 foundations in 123 countries of the world. Some of her sisters consider 1997 not the year of her death but as her 'birth into heaven'.

2000: Mother Teresa sisters return to Ireland to set up a convent in Sligo. The new convent was the congregation's gift to mark the millennium. Originally, the plan had been to open the new convent in Darjeeling where in 1946 Mother Teresa had experienced her call to follow Christ into the slums to serve Him among the poorest of the poor.

19 October 2003: As the autumn sun beamed down on the vast crowd in St Peter's Square in Rome, Mother Teresa was formally beatified by Pope John Paul II with the title Blessed Teresa of Calcutta. Following Mother Teresa's death the Holy See began the process of beatification, the first step towards possible canonisation, or sainthood. This process involves the documentation of a miracle. In 2002, the Vatican recognised as a miracle the healing of the tumour in the abdomen of an Indian woman, Monica Besra, following the application of Mother Teresa's picture to her body. Mrs Besra claimed that a beam of light

emanated from the picture, which cured the cancerous tumour.

A second miracle is needed for her canonisation.

The future: Each year, her feast day will be celebrated on the 5th of September.

Blessed Art Thou Amongst Men

A Tribute

'In the beginning was the word, and the word was NO!'
Thus began one of Brian Moore's short stories. This
sentence cleverly sums up the experience of those who
were brought up to see Catholicism in a painfully
negative way. To the many theology students in the Priory
Institute, Joe Kavanagh presented them with a very
different kind of Christianity. He appeared to favour an
approach espoused by Emily Brontë in 'Walking Out of
History':

> I'll walk, but not in old heroic traces
> And not in paths of high morality,
> And not among the half-distinguished faces,
> The clouded forms of long-past history.

I'll walk where my own nature would be leading:
It vexes me to choose another guide:
Where the grey flocks in ferny glens are feeding;
Where the wild wind blows on the mountain side.

What have those lonely mountains worth revealing?
More glory and more grief than I can tell:
The earth that wakes one human heart to feeling
Can centre both the worlds of Heaven and Hell.

As only the genuinely great teachers can do, he woke my
'heart to feeling'.

Preserving that cherished image remains important for
those who see it at first hand. His testimony of faith and
particularly his humanity, struck not so much a note of
hope as a symphony.

We do not have a great history in Ireland of a culture of

affirmation. We tend to wait until people die before we really salute their achievements. I wanted to use this book to pay a tiny tribute to a remarkable man who has made a significant contribution to Irish academic life and Irish Christianity.

In recent times a number of outstanding Irish people have had their lives and careers honoured by Festschrifts. Given his contribution to Irish life, I think Mother Teresa would agree it is indeed right and fitting that this volume honours the lifetime's work of Joe Kavanagh. This tribute is richly deserved and I am particularly pleased to count him as a friend. He personifies the exhortation on Mother Teresa's tombstone:

As I have loved you, you too love one another.

Prayer to Blessed Teresa of Calcutta

Blessed Teresa of Calcutta, Jesus called you to 'be His light', by loving and serving Him wholeheartedly in the poorest of the poor, and so satiating His thirst for love and souls.

Grant that I may also be, like you, a carrier of His light, love and peace to others, radiating His tender mercy to my brothers and sisters who live in darkness and pain.

Dear Mother Teresa, you promised to continue from heaven your mission of showing God's special love for those in need. With confidence, then, I entrust this intention to your care (state your petition).

Amen.